Favorite Zoo Animals
Book II

by

Marcia R. Pope

Copyright

Photography by Marcia R. Pope
Photographed on site Denver Zoo, Denver, Colorado

Published by
Marcia R. Pope
1975 E. 98th Ave.
Thornton, CO 80229
simpress1@hotmail.com

Table of Contents

This is an **Artic Fox**.
He has beautiful thick white fur in the
winter months. He can curl his tail
around himself to stay warm.
He likes to live under ground and
can hear very well.

The **African Crown Crane** has a long neck and body. Cranes like to eat insects, lizards, fish and seeds. The adult cranes sometimes do a graceful dance. Their wings can spread out to six feet wide.

Camels can weigh up to 1500 pounds. They can be up to 7 feet tall. They usually live in hot dry desert places. Camels can drink up to 40 gallons of water at one time. That's a lot of water!

The **Cattle Egret** can be found in
many parts of the world.
They love to eat insects like
grasshoppers and crickets.
They have white feathers and
hunched shoulders.
A group of egrets is called a
stampede.

The **African Cape Buffalo** lives in large herds. They like to eat hay and they are good swimmers.
They have good memories too.
They can be very vicious, so don't make them mad!

The male **Von der Decken's Hornbill**
bird has bright red and white bills.
Their feathers are black and white.
They can fly for only short distances.
They like to eat insects, fruit, seed,
crickets and mealworms.

Gorillas come mainly from Africa. This mother gorilla is caring for her baby. She keeps her baby close to her chest for about 2 months. After that, the baby gorilla holds onto the hairs on the mother's back until the baby is about 2 or 3 years old.

This is an **Egyptian Vulture**.
They are scavengers which means
they eat mostly small dead animals
and waste material.
They can fly long distances when
looking for food.

The **Komoto Dragon** is a type of
lizard but he is very big.
He can grow up to 10 feet long.
They are meat eaters.
They like to sit in the sun a lot too.

White Pelicans are big birds that can weigh up to 30 pounds.
Their wings can spread out for 9 feet when they fly.
They like to eat fish and sometimes they steal each other's food.

Lions live in a group called a pride.
This female lion is called a **Lioness**.
She is the main one who searches for
food. Lions can spend many hours just
resting and sleeping.
Baby lions are called cubs.
They love to play.

The **Gibbon Monkeys** lives mainly in trees. They are able to swing from one tree branch to another with no problem.
Unlike most monkeys, the Gibbon monkeys do not have a tail.

The **Red Panda Bear** is about the size of a house cat. He has a reddish-brown coat. Isn't he cute?
Red pandas like cold climates.
They eat mostly bamboo but sometimes they eat insects and fruit.

This animal is called an **Okapi**.
They are also called zebra giraffes.
They like to eat plants.
Did you know that their tongues are
long enough for them to lick
their own ears?

The **Rhinoceros Iguana** has very
rough scales on his skin.
He likes to eat leaves, fruit,
flowers and seeds.
Iguanas spend much of their day
resting in the sun.

The **Ruddy Shelduck** has beautiful rusty orange feathers. They are often found in lakes and rivers. They like to eat insects, fish, frogs and worms. They can make loud honking noises.

The **Siberian Tiger** is the largest of the cat family. He can weigh over 600 pounds. Look at his big paws! Tigers are very good hunters and swimmers. They can run about 50 miles an hour too.

These birds are called **Hawk-headed Parrots**. They can screech really loud. They like to play and sometimes they turn upside down just to show off. They make good pets.

Many types of fish can live in the same aquarium with no problem. The zoo has a large variety of very colorful fish of all sizes. This blue and yellow fish is called a **Naso Tang**. He can grow up to be 18 inches long.

The **Mongolian Wild Horse** is from
Mongolia and China. They spend most
of the day looking for food.
They live together in herds.
They like to eat grasses, shrubs
and other vegetation.
They have an excellent sense of
smell and hearing.

This tiny animal is called a
Mexican Leaf Frog.
He usually lives in warm tropical areas.
He is only about 4 inches long but
he can make very loud vocal sounds
ranging from low to high.

The **Rhinoceros** is a large animal.
He is called a Rhino for short.
His skin looks like armor. He is quite
content to be by himself.
Rhinos do not sweat, so they roll
around in the dust or mud when they
need to so they can keep cool.

Rainbow Lorikeets belong to
the parrot family.
Their feathers are beautiful colors
of red, blue, orange, yellow
and green. They like to be in
groups together and they
are very noisy.

This animal is called a **Zebra**. No two zebras are exactly alike because each one has his own special pattern of black and white stripes. Zebras stand up when they are sleeping. They eat mostly hay.

The **Gorilla** is a very intelligent animal.
He likes to eat fruit and leafy plants.
Gorillas can live for 35 to 40 years.
The male gorilla is twice the
size of the female gorilla.

The **Roseate Spoonbill** has bright
pink and white feathers.
The end of their beak is shaped like
a spoon and it helps them
to catch food. They eat small fish,
shrimp, insects and snails.
They are very sociable birds.

The End